www.providencebooks.net

Publisher Contact

Email:contact@providencebooks.net

Social media: facebook.com/providencebooks

Acknowledgements

The team at Providence Books would like to thank our friends, family, suppliers and customers for making our vision of creating the highest-quality books a reality. Thanks for purchasing and enjoy the quotes!

This page is intentionally left blank

This page is intentionally left blank

A Conservative Government is an organized hypocrisy.

Benjamin Disraeli

A University should be a place of light, of liberty, and of learning.

Benjamin Disraeli

A consistent soul believes in destiny, a capricious one in chance.

Benjamin Disraeli

A great city, whose image dwells in the memory of man, is the type of some great idea. Rome represents conquest; Faith hovers over the towers of Jerusalem; and Athens embodies the pre-eminent quality of the antique world, Art.

Benjamin Disraeli

A majority is always better than the best repartee.

Benjamin Disraeli

A man may speak very well in the House of Commons, and fail very completely in the House of Lords. There are two distinct styles requisite: I intend, in the course of my career, if I have time, to give a specimen of both.

Benjamin Disraeli

A precedent embalms a principle.

Benjamin Disraeli

Action may not always bring happiness; but there is no happiness without action.

Benjamin Disraeli

Adventures are to the adventurous.

Benjamin Disraeli

Almost everything that is great has been done by youth.

Benjamin Disraeli

An author who speaks about their own books is almost as bad as a mother who speaks about her own children.

Benjamin Disraeli

As a general rule, the most successful man in life is the man who has the best information.

Benjamin Disraeli

As for our majority... one is enough.

Benjamin Disraeli

Assassination has never changed the history of the world.

Benjamin Disraeli

Be amusing: never tell unkind stories; above all, never tell long ones.

Benjamin Disraeli

Beware of endeavoring to become a great man in a hurry. One such attempt in ten thousand may succeed. These are fearful odds.

Benjamin Disraeli

Change is inevitable. Change is constant.

Benjamin Disraeli

Characters do not change. Opinions alter, but characters are only developed.

Benjamin Disraeli

Circumstances are beyond human control, but our conduct is in our own power.

Benjamin Disraeli

Colonies do not cease to be colonies because they are independent.

Benjamin Disraeli

Conservatism discards Prescription, shrinks from Principle, disavows Progress; having rejected all respect for antiquity, it offers no redress for the present, and makes no preparation for the future.

Benjamin Disraeli

Courage is fire, and bullying is smoke.

Benjamin Disraeli

Damn your principles! Stick to your party.

Benjamin Disraeli

Despair is the conclusion of fools.

Benjamin Disraeli

Desperation is sometimes as powerful an inspirer as genius.

Benjamin Disraeli

Diligence is the mother of good fortune.

Benjamin Disraeli

Duty cannot exist without faith.

Benjamin Disraeli

Every man has a right to be conceited until he is successful.

Benjamin Disraeli

Every production of genius must be the production of enthusiasm.

Benjamin Disraeli

Everyone likes flattery; and when you come to Royalty you should lay it on with a trowel.

Benjamin Disraeli

Experience is the child of thought, and thought is the child of action.

Benjamin Disraeli

Fame and power are the objects of all men. Even their partial fruition is gained by very few; and that, too, at the expense of social pleasure, health, conscience, life.

Benjamin Disraeli

Fear makes us feel our humanity.

Benjamin Disraeli

Finality is not the language of politics.

Benjamin Disraeli

Frank and explicit - that is the right line to take when you wish to conceal your own mind and confuse the minds of others.

Benjamin Disraeli

Genius, when young, is divine.

Benjamin Disraeli

Great countries are those that produce great people.

Benjamin Disraeli

Grief is the agony of an instant; the indulgence of grief the blunder of a life.

Benjamin Disraeli

He was distinguished for ignorance; for he had only one idea, and that was wrong.

Benjamin Disraeli

How much easier it is to be critical than to be correct.

Benjamin Disraeli

I am prepared for the worst, but hope for the best.

Benjamin Disraeli

I have been ever of opinion that revolutions are not to be evaded.

Benjamin Disraeli

I have brought myself, by long meditation, to the conviction that a human being with a settled purpose must accomplish it, and that nothing can resist a will which will stake even existence upon its fulfillment.

Benjamin Disraeli

I must follow the people. Am I not their leader?

Benjamin Disraeli

I never deny. I never contradict. I sometimes forget.

Benjamin Disraeli

I repeat... that all power is a trust; that we are accountable for its exercise; that from the people and for the people all springs, and all must exist.

Benjamin Disraeli

I say that justice is truth in action.

Benjamin Disraeli

If a man be gloomy let him keep to himself. No one has the right to go croaking about society, or what is worse, looking as if he stifled grief.

Benjamin Disraeli

If you're not very clever you should be conciliatory.

Benjamin Disraeli

In a progressive country change is constant; change is inevitable.

Benjamin Disraeli

In politics nothing is contemptible.

Benjamin Disraeli

Increased means and increased leisure are the two civilizers of man.

Benjamin Disraeli

It destroys one's nerves to be amiable every day to the same human being.

Benjamin Disraeli

It is easier to be critical than correct.

Benjamin Disraeli

It is much easier to be critical than to be correct.

Benjamin Disraeli

Justice is truth in action.

Benjamin Disraeli

King Louis Philippe once said to me that he attributed the great success of the British nation in political life to their talking politics after dinner.

Benjamin Disraeli

Let the fear of a danger be a spur to prevent it; he that fears not, gives advantage to the danger.

Benjamin Disraeli

Life is too short to be little. Man is never so manly as when he feels deeply, acts boldly, and expresses himself with frankness and with fervor.

Benjamin Disraeli

Like all great travellers, I have seen more than I remember, and remember more than I have seen.

Benjamin Disraeli

Little things affect little minds.

Benjamin Disraeli

London is a modern Babylon.

Benjamin Disraeli

London is a roost for every bird.

Benjamin Disraeli

Man is made to adore and to obey: but if you will not command him, if you give him nothing to worship, he will fashion his own divinities, and find a chieftain in his own passions.

Benjamin Disraeli

Man is not the creature of circumstances, circumstances are the creatures of men. We are free agents, and man is more powerful than matter.

Benjamin Disraeli

Man is only great when he acts from passion.

Benjamin Disraeli

Mediocrity can talk, but it is for genius to observe.

Benjamin Disraeli

Moderation has been called a virtue to limit the ambition of great men, and to console undistinguished people for their want of fortune and their lack of merit.

Benjamin Disraeli

Moderation is the center wherein all philosophies, both human and divine, meet.

Benjamin Disraeli

My idea of an agreeable person is a person who agrees with me.

Benjamin Disraeli

My objection to Liberalism is this that it is the introduction into the practical business of life of the highest kind namely, politics of philosophical ideas instead of political principles.

Benjamin Disraeli

Nationality is the miracle of political independence; race is the principle of physical analogy.

Benjamin Disraeli

Nature, like man, sometimes weeps from gladness.

Benjamin Disraeli

Never apologize for showing feeling. When you do so, you apologize for the truth.

Benjamin Disraeli

Never complain and never explain.

Benjamin Disraeli

Never take anything for granted.

Benjamin Disraeli

Next to knowing when to seize an opportunity, the most important thing in life is to know when to forego an advantage.

Benjamin Disraeli

Nine-tenths of the existing books are nonsense and the clever books are the refutation of that nonsense.

Benjamin Disraeli

No Government can be long secure without a formidable Opposition.

Benjamin Disraeli

No man is regular in his attendance at the House of Commons until he is married.

Benjamin Disraeli

Nobody is forgotten when it is convenient to remember him.

Benjamin Disraeli

Nowadays, manners are easy and life is hard.

Benjamin Disraeli

Nurture your minds with great thoughts. To believe in the heroic makes heroes.

Benjamin Disraeli

One secret of success in life is for a man to be ready for his opportunity when it comes.

Benjamin Disraeli

Plagiarists, at least, have the merit of preservation.

Benjamin Disraeli

Power has only one duty - to secure the social welfare of the People.

Benjamin Disraeli

Read no history: nothing but biography, for that is life without theory.

Benjamin Disraeli

Real politics are the possession and distribution of power.

Benjamin Disraeli

Seeing much, suffering much, and studying much, are the three pillars of learning.

Benjamin Disraeli

Silence is the mother of truth.

Benjamin Disraeli

Something unpleasant is coming when men are anxious to tell the truth.

Benjamin Disraeli

Success is the child of audacity.

Benjamin Disraeli

Taking a new step, uttering a new word, is what people fear most.

Benjamin Disraeli

Talk to a man about himself and he will listen for hours.

Benjamin Disraeli

Teach us that wealth is not elegance, that profusion is not magnificence, that splendor is not beauty.

Benjamin Disraeli

That fatal drollery called a representative government.

Benjamin Disraeli

The Youth of a Nation are the trustees of posterity.

Benjamin Disraeli

The best security for civilization is the dwelling, and upon properly appointed and becoming dwellings depends, more than anything else, the improvement of mankind.

Benjamin Disraeli

The choicest pleasures of life lie within the ring of moderation.

Benjamin Disraeli

The difference between a misfortune and a calamity is this: If Gladstone fell into the Thames, it would be a misfortune. But if someone dragged him out again, that would be a calamity.

Benjamin Disraeli

The first magic of love is our ignorance that it can ever end.

Benjamin Disraeli

The fool wonders, the wise man asks.

Benjamin Disraeli

The governments of the present day have to deal not merely with other governments, with emperors, kings and ministers, but also with the secret societies which have everywhere their unscrupulous agents, and can at the last moment upset all the governments' plans.

Benjamin Disraeli

The greatest good you can do for another is not just to share your riches but to reveal to him his own.

Benjamin Disraeli

The health of the people is really the foundation upon which all their happiness and all their powers as a state depend.

Benjamin Disraeli

The more extensive a man's knowledge of what has been done, the greater will be his power of knowing what to do.

Benjamin Disraeli

The more you are talked about the less powerful you are.

Benjamin Disraeli

The palace is not safe when the cottage is not happy.

Benjamin Disraeli

The people of England are the most enthusiastic in the world.

Benjamin Disraeli

The practice of politics in the East may be defined by one word: dissimulation.

Benjamin Disraeli

The pursuit of science leads only to the insoluble.

Benjamin Disraeli

The right honourable gentleman caught the Whigs bathing, and walked away with their clothes. He has left them in the full enjoyment of their liberal positions, and he is himself a strict conservative of their garments.

Benjamin Disraeli

The secret of success in life is for a man to be ready for his opportunity when it comes.

Benjamin Disraeli

The secret of success is constancy to purpose.

Benjamin Disraeli

The secret of success is to be ready when your opportunity comes.

Benjamin Disraeli

The services in wartime are fit only for desperadoes, but in peace are only fit for fools.

Benjamin Disraeli

The very phrase 'foreign affairs' makes an Englishman convinced that I am about to treat of subjects with which he has no concern.

Benjamin Disraeli

The view of Jerusalem is the history of the world; it is more, it is the history of earth and of heaven.

Benjamin Disraeli

The wisdom of the wise and the experience of the ages are perpetuated by quotations.

Benjamin Disraeli

The world is governed by very different personages from what is imagined by those who are not behind the scenes.

Benjamin Disraeli

The world is weary of statesmen whom democracy has degraded into politicians.

Benjamin Disraeli

There are three kinds of lies: lies, damned lies, and statistics.

Benjamin Disraeli

There can be economy only where there is efficiency.

Benjamin Disraeli

There is moderation even in excess.

Benjamin Disraeli

There is no act of treachery or meanness of which a political party is not capable; for in politics there is no honour.

Benjamin Disraeli

There is no education like adversity.

Benjamin Disraeli

There is no gambling like politics.

Benjamin Disraeli

There is no greater index of character so sure as the voice.

Benjamin Disraeli

There is no index of character so sure as the voice.

Benjamin Disraeli

There is no waste of time in life like that of making explanations.

Benjamin Disraeli

Things must be done by parties, not by persons using parties as tools.

Benjamin Disraeli

Through perseverance many people win success out of what seemed destined to be certain failure.

Benjamin Disraeli

Time is precious, but truth is more precious than time.

Benjamin Disraeli

To be conscious that you are ignorant of the facts is a great step to knowledge.

Benjamin Disraeli

To supervise people, you must either surpass them in their accomplishments or despise them.

Benjamin Disraeli

To tax the community for the advantage of a class is not protection: it is plunder.

Benjamin Disraeli

Travel teaches toleration.

Benjamin Disraeli

Two nations between whom there is no intercourse and no sympathy; who are as ignorant of each other's habits, thoughts, and feelings, as if they were dwellers in different zones, or inhabitants of different planets. The rich and the poor.

Benjamin Disraeli

Upon the education of the people of this country the fate of this country depends.

Benjamin Disraeli

War is never a solution; it is an aggravation.

Benjamin Disraeli

We are all born for love. It is the principle of existence, and its only end.

Benjamin Disraeli

We cannot learn men from books.

Benjamin Disraeli

We moralize among ruins.

Benjamin Disraeli

We should never lose an occasion. Opportunity is more powerful even than conquerors and prophets.

Benjamin Disraeli

What is earnest is not always true; on the contrary, error is often more earnest than truth.

Benjamin Disraeli

What we anticipate seldom occurs: but what we least expect generally happens.

Benjamin Disraeli

When a man fell into his anecdotage it was a sign for him to retire from the world.

Benjamin Disraeli

Where knowledge ends, religion begins.

Benjamin Disraeli

William Gladstone has not a single redeeming defect.

Benjamin Disraeli

Without publicity there can be no public support, and without public support every nation must decay.

Benjamin Disraeli

Without tact you can learn nothing.

Benjamin Disraeli

Worry - a God, invisible but omnipotent. It steals the bloom from the cheek and lightness from the pulse; it takes away the appetite, and turns the hair gray.

Benjamin Disraeli

You can tell the strength of a nation by the women behind its men.

Benjamin Disraeli

You will find as you grow older that courage is the rarest of all qualities to be found in public life.

Benjamin Disraeli

Youth is a blunder; Manhood a struggle, Old Age a regret.

Benjamin Disraeli

This page is intentionally left blank

This page is intentionally left blank

This page is intentionally left blank

This page is intentionally left blank

This page is intentionally left blank

www.ingramcontent.com/pod-product-compliance
Lightning Source LLC
Chambersburg PA
CBHW061930280526
45787CB00004B/1547